Mary,
A Woman in Love

The Precious Apparitions
of Our Blessed Mother

By Franca Dornan

Art Illustrations by

Kathleen Auth
Cecilia Huckestein
Christine Mayer-Griese

Cover Design & Typeset by
Pluribus Media
Westlake Village, California

Contents

Mary
A Woman in Love

❧ Dedication ❧

I would like to dedicate this book to our beloved Blessed Mother who has given me the gift of Jesus and through her intercession, miracles in my life. With loving gratitude to my mama and papa, Oneglia and Andrea Bendi, who gave me life; such a beautiful, faith-filled life of deep affection. To my wonderful husband Dick, who is filled with Jesus' precious love, and shares it fervently with me, our family, and others. To my cherished children: Dick Jr., John, Tim, Gina, Patrick, my son-in-law Matthew, and our grand-daughters, Tyler and Gemma, who have enriched my heart with love, delight, meaning, and purpose. To my relatives, the Dornans and the Riccis, who through the years have given us much happiness and many joyous memories of Thanksgiving, Christmas and Easter celebrations.

To my special, dear friends and devoted prayer group Fiamus Sanctae, who have all given me their sweet friendship, a multitude of prayers, and many endearing moments. My dedication must also include: St. Jude the Apostle School, my Kindergarten classes, and Suzanne McHendry, who introduced me to the innocent world of children whom I could educate and guide into loving God, Jesus, and Our Blessed Mother; all the priests, Marymount nuns, and teachers in my life who inspired me to live our glorious faith; Kathleen Auth, Cecilia Huckestein, and Christine Mayer-Griese, whose expressive art has given life to my words; Jeannie Bouchard, whose inspiration has helped to make this book a reality; Roy and Simone Sparks, whose heartfelt prayers have given me spirit-filled wings which enabled me to soar in the beauty of writing about our revered Mother, Mary.

May all who read this book be touched with God's, Jesus' and Our Blessed Mother's immense affection for them so that they may love more, give more, become more, and lead others to Heaven.

 Foreword

...and the Word became flesh, and dwelt among us.

Nicene Creed

This phrase from the Nicene Creed, that we proclaim at every Sunday Mass, affirms the incarnation of Jesus when God entered into our human history as a real person. Jesus is called "the Word" in the Gospel of John because He is the ultimate expression and communication of God's love. All of this comes together in this beautiful book, by Franca Dornan. Her words affirm her great love for the woman by whom this incarnation took place. Her loving words reveal in wonderful detail the human person by whom the eternal Word entered into our world.

Several times in history Mary has made her presence felt, and some of the most famous moments are carefully outlined here in a series of chapters that reveal each as a profound historical event. The details of each story serve to affirm that Mary chose real people living in real places to present the Real Presence of Our Lord. Every appearance continues her role to present Her Son, the eternal Word, the expression of God's love for us, to people who are in great need to meet Him. Perhaps the appearance of Mary in Franca's home town of Rapallo, Italy, started her devotion that would one day culminate in the publication of this book that outlines Mary's appearances around the world.

In many of these miraculous appearances, the people to whom Mary appears are incredulous, surprised, and stunned. There is almost a universal reaction of "Why me?" Franca beautifully reveals how Mary lovingly and graciously assures each person that they are loved by God. Mary loves to bring the person of Jesus to everyone, and perhaps especially to those who least expect it. Franca clearly loves to tell her story!

Just as Mary brought to a waiting world the presence of Jesus, Franca has brought to us a most affectionate and beautiful portrait of a woman who continues to bring Our Lord to the whole world and to each of us.

Father Dave Heney
Pastor, St. Paschal Baylon
California, 2010

Rapallo, Italy

1 Our Lady appears to Giovanni Chichizola

2 Ceiling mural depicting 1557 apparition

3 The author in front of the basilica

4 View of Rapallo from Montallegro

5 Golden rederos with icon, at Our Lady of Montallegro

Preface

My precious faith, my beloved husband, treasured family, relatives, and friends are the breath of love and life in me. They are my joy in living. I love my God, my cherished Jesus, and my beautiful Blessed Mother with all my heart. I have written "Mary a Woman in Love" to awaken and inspire the beauty of faith in everyone. Our exquisite Mary has visited our earth in a magnificent tapestry of incredible apparitions to reveal God's eternal love for us. If we live Jesus' love, we will be embraced in His divine hug and wrapped in Our Blessed Mother's gentle, loving arms now and in eternity. What glorious company to share life with!

With all my love,

Franca Dornan

Mary Our Love

What a charming name for the most beautiful woman ever created. Mary is God's cherished love, Jesus' compassionate Mother, Joseph's endearing, faith-filled wife, and our caring, heavenly Mother.

Art by Christine Mayer-Griese

What a magnificent moment in time when Mary gave birth to Jesus in Bethlehem. The Divine plan, the miracle of the Incarnation was realized in a treasured baby boy who would teach the meaning of life by His very existence. The Divine became human and our earth was tenderly infused with an infinite and unfathomable love.

Mary nurtured Jesus in faith and tenderness, guided Him, cared for Him and taught Him Sacred Scripture. Jesus steadily grew in God's gentle ways and all-encompassing love. Our Blessed Mother prayed with Jesus and healed His wounds. Together they experienced the beauty of forgiveness, and God showered His grace upon them. Mary had the Savior of the world in her motherly care and bestowed upon Him infinite devotion.

Her love now stretches from Heaven to earth in a light that is blinding. It radiates and shimmers with abounding grace. One has only to accept her fondness and her heart explodes with joy.

Mary lives in God's marvelous embrace. She reveres Jesus who is the center of her life. The presence of the Holy Spirit enraptures her. Our exquisite Blessed Mother is totally surrounded, enveloped, and smothered in joy. Angels are her playmates. The saints caress her in divine bliss. The beauty of creation delights her. God's children sing to her and snuggle in her lap. It is everlasting happiness and ecstasy in Heaven, yet in one, miraculous moment, Mary appears to us. What a miracle! What passion! What does her heart reveal to her about her children that she descends upon us?

Our Mary is a woman who adores us. She is totally captivated with her Son, with the Holy Trinity, and with us. She wants us to experience Jesus' affection and be with our Divine Family forever. This is her story of touching earth, touching our hearts, to love Jesus more, live His blessed faith, and follow Him to Heaven.

Our Lady of Guadalupe

Tepeyac Hill has become one of the most famous hills in our Catholic story of Heaven touching earth. Juan Diego, a kind, fifty-seven-year old native from central Mexico had a rendezvous with the Mother of our Savior on this special hill. Juan was living in the small village of Tolpetlac, in the outskirts of Mexico City. At that time, the Aztec leaders' imposed their severe, pagan beliefs on everyone. With the coming of the Franciscan missionaries, who spread Jesus' love joyously, Juan and his charming Maria received the miracle of faith. Now they embraced a religion centered on love for God and His eternal love for them. Their new faith had become the essence of their existence. They had meaning and purpose in life, and Jesus found His home in their hearts.

Two years after Juan and Maria were baptized, Maria was called to Heaven. Juan experienced a deep sadness for his heart belonged to Maria. He had only his devoted uncle, Juan Bernardino, as part of his earthly family. With Jesus' love and consolation, Juan's faith grew and blossomed. His faith was like a tender, young rosebud unfolding into a beautiful rose. He lived to love Jesus and live His life.

Juan enjoyed going to Mass and receiving instruction in our revered Catholic faith. It was on a cold and chilly day, December 9, 1531, when an incredible miracle occurred that changed Juan's life forever. Juan was walking by Tepeyac Hill on his way to celebrate

Art by Cecilia Huckestein

Mass in Tlatelolco. This was a special Feast Day, the Feast of the Immaculate Conception, honoring our beloved Blessed Mother. As Juan was passing Tepeyac Hill, he heard the most blissful, tender music. He immediately thought it sounded like the singing of birds from Heaven. Their sound was melodious, soothing, and so inviting.

As he looked up to the top of the hill, he saw a most enchanting Lady standing on a small cloud surrounded by glittering light. Everything around this dazzling Lady shone with a rainbow of color reflecting the splendor of nature as if it were made of rare, multicolored jewels. Her expression was filled with kindness, peace, and love. She was wearing a flowing pink gown with a sash tied softly around her waist. A blue mantle dotted with golden stars laid gently on her head. Her demeanor was welcoming. The Lady had ebony hair and dark eyes of affection. She resembled a delicate, Aztec princess.

Suddenly this vision of loveliness spoke to Juan. The Lady said, "My dear Juan, my dearest Juan Diego!" As she called his name, Juan quickly climbed the hill to be near this graceful Lady. She asked a further question, "My precious son, where are you going?" Juan told her that he was going to Mass and wanted to learn from the priests more about his cherished faith. Then in the next moment she said,

"Know and be certain in your heart, my precious son, that I am the Ever Virgin Holy Mary, Mother of the One, True God, Who created Heaven and Earth." Did Juan really hear these sacred words? Could they be true?

Mary descends upon earth and gives us gifts of love and miracles occur. Juan Diego felt he was in a wonderful dream. Was this miracle really happening to him? Was our loving Blessed Mother appearing to a poor Indian? Our devoted Mary saw the affection in Juan's heart and filled him with her grace. Juan experienced an intense, burning love for Mary and her Son, Jesus. She spoke again and told him of her wish to have a church built on Tepeyac Hill where she could show her love, and sweet compassion for everyone who needed her. She wanted to console her loved ones and always be there for them in times of trouble and sorrow. Juan was to go to the Bishop of Mexico, Bishop Zumarraga, with her sincere request.

Juan was enthralled with what had just occurred. The Mother of Jesus had appeared to him and had requested that he speak to this noble dignitary of the church about her passionate dream. He had Heaven's love before him, beside him, and within him. Would the bishop believe that he, Juan Diego, had seen and spoken with Our Blessed Mother?

To please this glorious Lady was Juan's desire. He gathered his courage and visited the bishop on three occasions. Bishop Zumarraga was hesitant in believing Juan and on the second visit asked him if the Lady would give him a sign, showing that she was truly the Mother of God. Juan relayed the message to his alluring Lady. She agreed and asked Juan to return the next day and the sign would be given. What a moving moment for Juan to be able to have proof of Our Mother Mary's appearances to him.

That evening Juan's uncle, Juan Bernardino, became quite ill and needed a priest. Our devoted Indian with a saddened heart couldn't meet his Lady the next day for his uncle was dying. On his journey to find a priest, Mary appeared to Juan and said that his uncle was well. He was overcome with joy. She then said to Juan, "Go to the top of Tepeyac Hill. There you will find flowers growing. Gather as many as you can and place them in your tilma and bring them to me." Juan did as Our Lady asked. At the top of the hill, in very rocky, arid soil, radiant Castilian roses were blooming. Their fragrant scent was overpowering. Juan was astonished that these stunning roses were in blossom in winter. He quickly gathered them and placed them in his tilma. Juan showed them to Our Blessed Mother and with her gentle hands she arranged them delicately in his course, cactus cloth tilma.

Mary was so pleased with the attractive bouquet of roses and said, "Go now to the bishop. Tell him this is the sign he asked from me in order to fulfill my desire. Today the bishop will believe you." Juan was filled with excitement and wanted to please Our Lady very much. He hurried to the palace of the bishop and anxiously waited to see him. Bishop Zumarraga welcomed Juan and asked what was in his tilma? Juan opened his tilma and let the sweet-scented, Castilian roses fall gently to the floor. The bishop was filled with joy and wonder for imprinted on Juan's tilma was a breathtaking, miraculous image of our precious Blessed Mother. Her face looked like a beautiful, Indian princess with loving eyes revealing her heart. Juan then looked surprisingly at his tilma and was overwhelmed for upon it was his love, Our Mary. This was the miraculous sign. What a sign to last through the ages. A portrait of Our Blessed Lady was emblazoned on his tilma by divine intervention.

The bishop loved Our Blessed Mother with a deep intensity. He immediately had a church built on Tepeyac Hill in her honor. Now her requests were fulfilled. People from everywhere could come to show their love for Jesus and ask her for her caring, compassion, protection, and intercession in their needs.

Juan's uncle also had a visit from God's loving Mary. He had been healed through her intercession. She asked that the church to be built on Tepeyac Hill be named Our Lady of Guadalupe, and so it was! Juan's tilma, with the image of Mary, was placed above the main altar for all to venerate and love. Juan Diego's ravishing Mother would be forever present for him and for all her children. For the rest of his life, Juan was caretaker of his church where his Jesus and his Blessed Mother live and have their home. An amazing eight million Indians, in the course of seven years, fell in love with our Catholic faith. They were baptized due to the miracle of Our Lady of Tepeyac.

As the years unfolded, a magnificent basilica to Our Lady of Guadalupe was built on Tepeyac Hill in Mexico City to welcome the incredible amount of visitors. About 14 million pilgrims have come each year to view the miraculous tilma and to show their love and gratitude to Our Blessed Mother. Her message to the world was one of everlasting love and compassion for her dear ones, and she gives us that message today. Many miracles have occurred through her intercession to her Son, Jesus. Churches in Mexico are filled with people attending Mass, receiving reconciliation, and Holy Eucharist. Many continued conversions to our Catholic faith have taken place. Our faith is reverently lived. Juan's tilma, after hundreds of years, has not deteriorated and Mary's miraculous image is as beautiful as ever.

Do you feel God's amazing love for us radiating from the love of His Mother, Mary? Our Blessed Mother appears to us, touches us, transforms us, and rekindles Jesus' love and presence within us. Then she leaves us in awe to divinely soar in our faith. What esteemed gifts she has given us!

Art by Kathleen Auth

K. AUTH

Our Lady of Montallegro

On the Italian Riviera, the charming town of Rapallo rests peacefully against the green expansive Mediterranean. It is famous for its promenade lined with impressive palm trees and numerous prestigious hotels. To the north of Rapallo lies Santa Margherita Ligure, an elegant resort, with frequent sailing races and aquatic adventures. The pearl of the Riviera is the delightful town of Portofino, once a fisherman's alcove. The Piazzetta has attractive boutiques, art galleries, and glamorous restaurants. The marina is filled with yachts and many little boats dotting the blue, engaging horizon. To the south of Rapallo lies Cinque Terre which is the name given to five quaint, fascinating towns: Monterosso, Vernazza, Corniglia, Manarola, and Riomaggiore. These scenic villages are built either on top of low rugged mountains or built into its countryside. Vineyard terraces can be seen along the path, Via dell' Amore, which connects them all. The delicious aroma of the Italian cuisine, and the sweet taste of Asti Spumante, entices welcome guests to enjoy Cinque Terre's gourmet restaurants. European warmth radiates everywhere. This is the life and lavish surroundings in the present day of the beautiful Italian Riviera situated on the Ligurian coast.

In the year 1557, the natural beauty of this region existed in its pure, pristine form. Rapallo, the town in the center of all this loveliness, was touched and transformed by the radiant Queen from

Heaven. It happened on July 2ⁿᵈ of that year. Rapallo became the setting of a miracle where Our Blessed Mother gave intense spiritual blessings to this area. Our Mary knows where and when to appear to bring the love of her Son to others.

Giovanni Chichizola, an Italian farmer, was working on a mountain high above Rapallo named Montallegro, which means "Happy Mountain." What an appropriate name for the mountain that would be graced by Our Mother of Joy. Giovanni decided to take a little reprieve from his job. As he was resting, he suddenly heard his name gently being called. A Lady was beside him. Who was this enchanting vision? He had never seen anyone with so much love emanating from her presence. He was only a peasant. How could he be touched by such compassion? Then in a splendid moment, the vision spoke again. He felt he was in another world. He experienced such excitement. "Don't be afraid Giovanni. I am Mary, the Mother of God. Tell the people in Rapallo that you have seen me." Did he hear what he thought he heard? Was this truly God's Mother and why would she appear to him? His heart was beating with love.

Our Blessed Mother asked Giovanni to have a church built and she also showed him an icon of her Assumption. She said it had been transported to the mountain from Greece by angels. How miraculous! Giovanni could see Our Lady, as if she were sleeping on a bed, and rising to Heaven as a child. Above her, three human faces merged into one. To the left of Our Blessed Mother, Peter was holding the Book of Scripture, to her right were some apostles and disciples in wonder, at the top of the icon were angels hovering over this incredible scene. This was all so overwhelming and spectacular.

What a magnificent painting revealing the blessed beliefs of our faith: the Assumption, the Trinity, Peter as Pope and head of our Catholic Church—several apostles, the first priests, the disciples, the followers of Jesus and angels watching over us and protecting us.

Giovanni tried to pick up this sacred icon but it was firmly attached to a rock. A stream of water began to flow from underneath the rock. Was it a natural spring or one from Heaven? This was very extraordinary. He had to share his marvelous encounter.

Excitedly, Giovanni ran down the mountainside into the town of Rapallo and told the parish priests the incredible meeting with our dearly loved Mother. They didn't believe his mystical story. However, several priests returned with Giovanni to Montallegro, to the spot he had spoken of. They were astonished, for there in obvious view was the treasured icon. They were able to release the icon from the rock, and they carried it with reverence in procession to their church. It was securely placed under lock and key so that no one would have access to it. This was truly a remarkable experience.

What a night filled with thoughts of Our Blessed Mother and our loving faith, and it all happened in Rapallo. Giovanni was filled with grace and joy. Did his eyes really witness the Mother of Jesus? Had she really given him this picture of her life proclaiming her Assumption? His heart knew it was all so true for he had experienced infinite love. The next morning, the archpriest went to look at the icon and it wasn't there where the priest had gently and ever so carefully placed it. He and the other priests looked and looked without success. They finally went up to Montallegro and the icon was found where Our Blessed Mother had given it to our humble Giovanni. It was then decided that Our Lady wanted her picture there in that exact place. A shrine was built to give honor to our precious Mother and love to her Son, Jesus. Eventually a beautiful church was constructed in that attractive setting high above the ocean. The church was given the title, "Our Lady of Montallegro."

An interesting account related to Our Lady of Montallegro concerned a sailing vessel that was almost shipwrecked by turbulent storms. The captain prayed to Our Blessed Mother to save his men and his ship. If she performed this miracle, he and his crew would go the nearest sanctuary to give her honor. They were saved and the nearest church was in Rapallo. The captain and the sailors climbed the mountain, and in the sanctuary they gave Our Lady love, praise, and thanks. As they prayed, they saw the icon and believed it was theirs taken from their town, Ragusa, now known as Dubrovnik, Croatia.

The matter was taken to court and the judge decided in their favor. The people of Rapallo were devastated. The captain and his crew left happily on their ship and as they were rounding Portofino, the icon mysteriously disappeared. It was discovered back on top of the mountain and it is there to this day, in the church overlooking the Italian Riviera. The people of Rapallo were thrilled, for they loved Our Blessed Mother with all their hearts. They were enthralled with Mary's icon that they wanted it to remain with them forever.

Our Lady of Montallegro Church, in time, was given the honor of being named a basilica. It is a charming, white, picturesque basilica. Inside, on the ceiling above the main altar, is a painting of Our Lady gracing Giovanni with her presence. He is kneeling in humility to her. It is a tender, captivating scene.

The prized icon is reverently displayed in a magnificent, golden rederos behind the high altar. The significance of the rock once touched by Mary's icon was strategically placed in the structure of this unique church. In a special room is an attractive white marble basin into which Mary's bubbling spring gently flows. Many pilgrims come to fill containers with this valued water, and miracles have occurred from this blessed spring.

People from all over the world visit Our Blessed Mother's Basilica. Masses are joyously said. Jesus is received in the miracle of the Holy Eucharist. Countless confessions, reconciliations, and conversions occur. Weddings take place overlooking the splendid bay. Rapallo has been saved several times from the plague. What fantastic miracles to be graced on this Riviera town. Our Mother of Love sent Jesus' healing to this land of hope and joy. In 1739, Our Lady of Montallegro became the patroness of Rapallo. She is revered and venerated. Our dear Mary has blessed the people of Rapallo and the world with her presence. Her dream is for everyone to center their lives on her Son Jesus, and live His sacred teachings.

The natural beauty of the Riviera is breathtaking, but it pales in comparison to the spiritual beauty of the quaint, white basilica where Our Blessed Mother is cherished and her Son is adored. Faith and divinity captures our hearts and souls. Once touched by God's grace flowing from Our Blessed Mary, comes surrender to her total love. Once touched by Jesus through Mary, comes a desire to live only for our dear faith. Spiritual blessings overwhelm your total being.

I happened to be born in Rapallo and have visited this majestic basilica several times. You feel as if you are in Heaven, high above the world. The sky seems a brighter blue. The sun's rays seem more golden. The ocean below shines and glimmers endlessly. Birds dance to the music of the wind.

Our Lady lives there with her Son and they truly bless all who come to ask for their help. Jesus waits for you. He wants to enter your heart. He wants you to fall more and more in love with Him and with His Mother. Then your life will be filled with deep faith and contentment. To receive Jesus in Holy Communion at Our Lady of Montallegro is to experience Heaven. Come to Rapallo and come to Our Mary's home and become spiritually refreshed and loved for the miracle of love that you are.

Art by Kathleen Auth

K.Auth

Our Lady of the Miraculous Medal

In the quaint village of Fain-lès-Moutiers, Burgundy, France, a charming little baby girl was born. She was a beautiful miracle from Heaven and her birthday, May 2, 1806, will forever remain in our hearts. Her entrance into our world had profound significance as she matured and became a vehicle of grace for God. She was christened Catherine but was called Zoé due to being born on the special feast day of St. Zoé. She was a precious blessing to the Labourés who already were gifted with a large family. At the age of nine, Zoé experienced the loss of her dear mother which devastated her and her loving family. The beauty of faith encircled them, and they continued living their daily lives with the love of their mother embedded in their hearts.

Zoé loved Our Blessed Mother immensely. She wanted to be embraced by her and become her loving child now that her mother was in the arms of God. In a tender moment, Zoé was found hugging a statue of Our Lady, and announcing with fervent emotion that now she would be her mother. What a splendid thought, for truly our heavenly Mother is our Mother of caring and devotion. This young, innocent nine-year-old child could now face life being wrapped in Our Lady's love.

As the years evolved, Zoé blossomed in her faith. She attended Mass a few days a week and fell more and more in love with Jesus and

His Blessed Mother. Zoé was like the white iris surrounded by violet irises in Vincent Van Gogh's painting titled, "The Irises." She had a delicate individual quality about her. Her faith was lived in joy and she seemed to stand out differently from the rest of the world. She was the white iris living her faith in a wounded world. Her vocation to enter the convent of the Daughters of Charity in Paris grew in her soul.

Once God touches you with divine charm, you are His for eternity.

Zoé Catherine's dream became a beautiful reality in January 1830 when she entered the hospice of the Daughters of Charity, at Châtillon-sur-Siene. A few months later in April, Catherine entered the novitiate at their mother house on the Rue du Bac, in Paris. What a glorious moment in her life to have her heart's desires fulfilled at her young age of twenty-four. To become a bride of Jesus and have His heart and Catherine's heart melt into one must be a blessed, experience! And it was hers to enjoy in ecstasy! Now Zoé became known as Sister Catherine and reveled in her life as a nun. Our lovely Blessed Mother had myriads of graces to be bestowed on God's children; in a short time, Sister Catherine was chosen to be the instrument of her love.

Our delightful nun had a most wonderful encounter with divine bliss on the evening of July 18, 1830. The nuns had retired and were sleeping. Suddenly, a young boy about five-years-old awakened Sister Catherine. He seemed to glow interiorly with a magical brightness. The startled nun thought it might possibly be her special guardian angel. Then in a magnificent moment, he said, "Come to the chapel. The Blessed Virgin awaits you." Sister Catherine could hardly breathe from excitement.

Her Mother of Love, whom she revered, was here on the Rue du Bac, in the Daughters of Charity convent and wanted to see her.

Our charming nun's head was dizzy with affection as she followed the young angel. The corridor was aglow with many twinkling lights. As Sister Catherine entered the chapel, it was ablaze with dazzling, shimmering candles. It looked like the beauty of Christmas everywhere. It was a spectacular sight but not compared to what our Sister experienced next.

The angel told her to kneel next to the chaplain's chair. In the quiet of the moment, a rustling sound of silk could be heard. Then a most exquisite Lady sat in the chaplain's chair. It was Our Blessed Mother appearing to Sister Catherine, close to the hour of midnight. What a miracle! Heaven's love was in the chapel. Sister Catherine knelt at her feet and placed her hands gently in Our Lady's lap. Profound joy overwhelmed her, and the pure ecstasy of faith filled her soul. For two welcomed hours, Our Lady conversed with our sweet Catherine. Imagine looking and listening to the Mother who gave birth to Jesus, adored him, and loves us as well. Catherine was in rapture.

Our Blessed Mother told Catherine that Jesus deeply loved her. What a divine thought! Her heart exploded with delight. Our Lady continued and stated that she had a mission for Catherine and it would be revealed to her at a later date. Our Blessed Lady said that prayer is so needed when sorrow delves into our hearts. She sadly mentioned in tears the tragedies that were to touch France and religious orders. It was imperative for everyone to come to our holy altar and pray, for through prayer, graces would be abundantly given. It was an intimate meeting filled with extreme love and sorrow. Then Our Lady left and Catherine's heart was broken with her tears and sad prophecies.

Catherine told only one person of her meeting, Father Aladel, who did not believe her. Her secret meeting with our compassionate Blessed Mother was kept solely in her heart. She knew her dear

Mother had a purpose for her, and she anxiously awaited her mission. Catherine continued her duties and studies as a young nun.

Some of the tragedies that would touch France sadly occurred shortly after our Mary's predictions. King Charles was overthrown by an enraged citizenry who felt their freedoms and rights were taken away. Religious orders received the backlash of their anger. It was the saddest of times in a Catholic country. In time, King Louis Philippe garnered the throne as a figurehead king, and France experienced a period of peace.

Life on the Rue du Bac was lived as usual with our faith-filled nuns loving their God and God's children and performing acts of charity. On the evening of Nov. 27, 1830, during evening prayers and meditation, another extraordinary miracle occurred. Catherine was reflecting on a special reading when that wonderful sound of silk or taffeta was heard. Could it be Our Lady once again inspiring, loving, and appearing to her daughter? As Catherine looked to the right of the altar, there was the vision of splendor.

It was Our Blessed Mother dressed in white silk with a delicate, long white veil. Mary was standing on a globe, with her foot on a coiled snake, holding a golden ball in her hands. She seemed to be offering it to our dear Father in Heaven as her adoring eyes were looking upwards. Her hands had rings with precious gems which radiated dazzling rays on the globe below. The uniqueness of the rays was that only some were shining brightly from the gems while others were devoid of resplendent radiance.

Our Mary spoke to Catherine's gentle heart and related that the golden ball represented our earthly world, France in particular, and each one of us. The rays signified graces given to those who requested them. The gems that did not shine and exude rays represented the people who did not ask for the blessed gift of grace. How sad for some not to receive such precious grace. Catherine was in total astonishment at what was happening. The vision changed once more. Our exquisite Blessed Mother was graciously standing on the earth below without the golden globe. Her arms and hands were pointing downward with her palms opened toward Catherine, as if to embrace her loved ones. Shimmering rays were also cascading from her hands. What a divine scene! An oval border formed around Our Lady with these magnificent words.

"Oh Mary conceived without sin,

Pray for us who have recourse to you."

In Mary's own words speaking to Catherine's heart she said, "Have a medal struck after this model. All who wear it will receive great graces; they shall wear it around their necks. Graces will abound for persons who wear it with confidence." Then, the next moment, the other side of the medal came into view. A large 'M' with a cross above it was intertwined on a bar. Beneath the bar were the sacred hearts of our precious Jesus and our cherished Mary; Jesus' blessed heart surrounded with thorns and Mary's loving heart with a sword piercing it; two hearts filled with such profound love for us. Twelve stars encircled the scene.

Now Catherine knew her mission—to have a medal made and to have the people of the world wear this dearest medal in honor of Our Blessed Mother. Then a multitude of spiritual graces would be given to all who believed in our beloved Mary's words. Catherine thought that this was a mission of destiny, and she was ready to do everything to succeed with Our Lady's request.

It took about two years before the blessed medal was made. Our devoted Mother had appeared several times to Sister Catherine to have

Father Aladel proceed with its production. With the most welcomed approval of the Archbishop of Paris, permission was finally granted. Catherine was thrilled. In June 1832, fifteen hundred holy medals of Our Mary finally became a reality. Our Lady of Grace must have been sending kisses from Heaven for her desire was accomplished. The Medal of the Immaculate Conception was given to her dear children. By 1836, millions of Mary's medals were produced and dispersed throughout the world.

As people wore this spiritual medal, overflowing graces radiated in their souls. Miracles, conversions, healings, and a renewed faith occurred. The medal became known as the Miraculous Medal due to its miraculous, healing graces. Jesus heals through the graces showered by Our Blessed Mother.

Our Lady loves us so much that she is constantly giving us means to attain a faith-filled life on earth, and then leading us to Heaven. What a precious gift in so small a medal! I wear the lovely Miraculous Medal around my neck, and I constantly kiss Our Lady of Love; Our Mary, Our Mother who had divine Jesus in her womb, Our Eternal Mother of caring and affection. Miracles surround us every day. Just look and see the miracle of faith and life in you!

Sister Catherine put a fabulous smile on Mary's face and sweet love in her heart for she answered Mary's call, and the world became a better place. The remainder of her life was spent taking care of the dear elderly at Enghiens, a hospice near her convent. Our gentle Lord welcomed Catherine home on Dec. 31, 1876 at age 70. Catherine Labouré was proclaimed a saint on July 27, 1947. As part of her sainthood, her body had to be exhumed. Another magnificent miracle occurred! Catherine was as beautiful as ever. She was completely preserved! Our devoted saint can be viewed at the Daughters of Charity convent, at 40 Rue du Bac, looking youthful.

Catherine had such a deep love for Jesus and Our Blessed Mother that it overflowed in her soul. She is now giving her love of Jesus and Mary to us. We just have to breathe it in and live it. Belief in our faith is a gift of love. If we love our faith with all our hearts, the splendid company of the Trinity and our Blessed Mary are ours! They will live joyously in us as they did in Sister Catherine Labouré!

Treasure the Miraculous Medal given to us by our charming Blessed Mother to Sister Catherine. Wear it around your neck and receive the abundance of grace gifted to us by God through His love, Our Mary! The most precious gift one can receive is the gift of Love. Grace is a magnificent gift of Love. It is ours to enjoy and be immersed in!

Art by Kathleen Auth

Our Lady of Lourdes

Lourdes is a small, picturesque village in the Pyrenees in France. It is surrounded by natural beauty. Rolling mountains majestically crown the countryside. Trees sway and dance to the ebb and flow of the changing seasons. God's artistic touch can be seen everywhere. It is Feb. 11, 1858, and this is the setting of a miracle that would change the world forever and radiate love to every corner of the earth.

It all began in the humble home of Francois Soubirous. He and his wife were people of deep faith who loved their children immensely. Mr. Soubirous had lost his flour mill which had been a source of income for his family. They both worked hard and accepted any job to support their children. This was a difficult time in their lives, but they endured their hardship with dignity and love.

The village had experienced a light snowstorm, and the air was filled with a bitter cold. The Soubirous needed bundles and bundles of firewood to warm their modest home. Fourteen-year-old Bernadette, her younger sister, Toinette, and their friend, Jeanne, set on a little adventure to collect the much needed wood. They enjoyed playing and being together. The girls loved having fun and this chore was one of delight for them. They talked and sang as they made their way through their little village and headed for a spot filled with kindling wood.

They finally reached the chilly River Gave where its surroundings are known to be overflowing with lots of twigs. Toinette and Jeanne rushed excitedly into the cold river and anxiously crossed to the other side. They dashed off to find as much firewood as possible. Bernadette, having had asthma as a young child and still experiencing it, was quite hesitant to cross the frigid, uninviting river. She was sad that she could not run after her playmates. Suddenly, she heard the rustle of wind. The tree branches and leaves surrounding her were absolutely still. Why weren't they swaying with the wind? The atmosphere was filled with a quiet serenity. This was so strange, so very unusual. In a dramatic moment, Bernadette was drawn to look in the direction of the Grotto at Massabielle.

There in the grotto, Bernadette saw the most beautiful Lady she had ever seen. Bernadette's heart began to pound louder and louder as if it would burst. The excitement was overwhelming. Bernadette was entranced with this apparition of splendor. The Lady was dressed completely in white with a white veil and a blue sash. Pretty, pale yellow roses gently rested on her feet. She was holding a Rosary, also light in color, draped over her hand. The engaging Lady smiled with so much genuine love and affection, and then she made the sign of the cross. Bernadette immediately fell to her knees and began praying the mysteries of the Rosary that her loving parents had taught her. Bernadette was filled with love. She was in ecstasy! Who was this captivating Lady? Was she from Heaven? Was she Jesus' Mother, Our Blessed Mother? Bernadette didn't know who she was but only felt her immense love, her profound presence. It seemed as if their tender hearts melted into one. What a feeling of bliss!

Toinette and Jeanne returned happily with their firewood. They had a wonderful adventure but it didn't compare to the miraculous experience that Bernadette encountered. They never were gifted with the appearance of the mysterious Lady. Bernadette secretly told

Toinette of her amazing vision which, in her enthusiasm, Toinette told family and friends. Bernadette was not believed and was made fun of, but she knew the Lady was a reality and had pierced her heart with love.

Our Lady had requested that Bernadette return to the grotto and she did in great anticipation. She was graced with eighteen visits with this vision of everlasting love. Bernadette was in awe in the presence of this charming apparition. Together they continued to share the spiritual beauty of saying our cherished Rosary. The Lady asked Bernadette to kiss the ground, drink and wash from the spring, and eat of the plant nearby. Bernadette obeyed the gentle Lady. She kissed the ground, looked for a spring but no water was in sight. She ate the uninviting plant and dug vigorously into the soil. In time, a marvelous little spring emerged, a miraculous spring. A multitude of miracles ensued from this supernatural spring given to Bernadette and the world. Another request was to have a chapel built and have people come in procession. The effect of having a chapel would result in Masses being said. Blessings, healings, conversions would occur through the miracle of the Holy Eucharist. This virtuous Lady could only be the Blessed Mother of Jesus for she knew how to win hearts for our beloved Savior.

Then in an endearing moment, on the twenty-fifth of March, the Feast of the Annunciation, the Lady revealed who she was. Heaven and earth rejoiced hearing her hallowed name, "I am the Immaculate Conception." These words revealed that it was Mary, God's love, the Mother of Jesus, God's gift of love to us. The only person ever conceived free of original sin. What a breathtaking revelation. It touched the heart of the Catholic world with an explosion of majesty, splendor, and the reality of our faith.

This was Our Mary, Queen of Heaven, and Queen of Our Hearts as she appeared to young Bernadette giving her the gift of the wondrous miracle spring and the knowledge of her conception free from original sin. This confirmed her Blessed and Sacred Motherhood of her Divine Son, Jesus. What an announcement! It would be echoed to us through eternal time. Bernadette was now believed, since a young, uneducated girl would not have known these spiritual words, "I am the Immaculate Conception" or their marvelous meaning. Bernadette had not even made her First Holy Communion due to helping her mother care for their family. In a short while, she would receive this precious sacrament. On that day, the miracle of Jesus in the Holy Eucharist would be physically present in her heart. For now, he lived there spiritually, because Bernadette was very holy.

Bernadette saw the Blessed Mother two more times. Then on July 16, 1858, Mary gloriously returned to God's Divine embrace, but the memory of those splendid visits remained forever in her pure heart. Bernadette was filled with an overwhelming love and affection for her lovely Lady in White. Her life on earth was sustained by this sacred love. Imagine a young girl of fourteen having the Queen of Heaven to converse with her! Miracles do happen and they happened to this humble, young girl whose heart and soul belonged to Jesus.

The years ahead held many emotions of joy and sorrow. Bernadette, once having experienced Mary's love only wanted to be with her forever. In time, she became a Sister of Charity at Nevers and took gentle care of the sick. The youthful nun devoted the rest of her life to her loves: the Blessed Trinity and Mary. She returned to their loving arms at the tender age of thirty-five. On Dec. 8, 1933, on the Feast of the Immaculate Conception, Bernadette was made a saint! What a splendid honor to be recognized as a saint on that magnificent Feast! Her heart must have been fluttering with love in Heaven above and in her joy, showering blessings on us.

A chapel was built at the grotto in Lourdes, and later another church and basilica were added. People from all over the world have come to experience Mary's love, compassion, and affection for her Son and for us. Masses are said daily, and Jesus is lovingly and reverently received in the Holy Eucharist. Miracles, spiritual and physical, take place in the miraculous spring given to us by Jesus, through His Mother. The procession of the Blessing of the Sick, with Jesus in the Holy Monstrance, is filled with devotion. The Stations of the Cross, on the scenic hillside, are prayed with such dignity and reverence. The significance and beauty of the mysteries of the Rosary grows in peoples' hearts. They are prayed in candle-light procession with everyone giving love and honor to our Heavenly Family.

Mary's requests were graciously granted. She is truly a woman in love with Jesus and with us. From the beginning of time, God knew Mary was needed for her miraculous, Divine Motherhood, and to continuously inspire us to love Jesus. By His presence, His sacred teachings, and His death on the cross, Jesus would redeem us and lead us to the purpose for which we were born—Heaven.

Art by Cecilia Huckestein

Our Lady of Fatima

The spring of 1916 held immense wonders that were so extraordinary. The setting was the country of Portugal. The scene of divine blessings took place in the little farming village of Aljustrel. Three amusing children who loved Jesus and Mary very much were leading their sheep to pasture in the neighboring fertile hillsides. Lucia de Jesus, nine-years-old and the eldest, was quite mature and very bright. She took very good care of her two cousins, and they loved being with her. Francisco, eight-years-old, was sweet and gentle. He had a tender heart and was fascinated with the beauty of God's gifts in nature: dawn, sunrise and sunset. Jacinta, the six-year-old, was very fragile and impressionable and had a sweet fondness for her little, gentle sheep. These innocent children were so loved by God. They would probably be the first ones to sit on Jesus' lap if Jesus appeared in the present day and said, "Let the little children come to me." They would race to see who would get there first.

These joyous children were bonded in love to each other and to their faith. They had the presence of Jesus in their hearts. Every day they would say the Rosary, the short version. The title "Our Father" was recited once, and the title "Hail Mary" was said ten times and the title "Glory Be" was said once, and so on, until the five decades of the Rosary were hopefully completed. It was fun praying this way and very quick also. It wouldn't be long before these pure children would be reciting the Rosary in its entirety. They were delightful young people overflowing with love and fervent faith.

One day, as they were tending their flocks, a gentle rain began to fall. They found shelter in a cozy cave. In the afternoon, a strong wind arose and a bright light approached them, becoming more sparkling. Their hearts were exploding with wonder. The light surrounded a celestial angel who stood before them. What a valuable moment in their sweet lives to be in the presence of an angel. This magnificent being sent from God said, "Do not be afraid, I am the Angel of Peace. Pray with me. Pray like this. The hearts of Jesus and Mary are attentive to your supplications. My God, I believe, I adore, I hope, and I love you. I beg pardon for all who do not believe, do not adore, do not hope, and do not love you." In the next moment, he disappeared into the heavens.

The children were brimming with excitement. It was a euphoric moment for them. They would pray this sacred prayer faithfully, for Jesus was the center of their young lives. Their heavenly guest appeared two more times asking them to pray, and offer sacrifice for the conversion of sinners. The angel requested this, for their hearts were so virtuous that they could be carried on his wings to Heaven instantly. Yet Jesus needed their prayers and little sacrifices to save others. In his last appearance, the three children received the greatest gift of all, Jesus in Holy Communion. What a thrilling moment to receive Jesus from an angel, the Angel of Peace. These little shepherds experienced sublime love. Their futures were held in Jesus' hands. How blessed they were!

About one year later, on the thirteenth of May 1917, God's Divine plan unfolded. Lucia, Francisco, and Jacinta were tending their sheep at the Cova da Iria on a bright, sunny day. Suddenly a streak of lightning shot across the sky. A quiet stillness followed, and then another blinding light which overwhelmed them. The three little shepherds were speechless. They looked towards a holmoak tree and they saw a most magnificent Lady clothed in brilliant light floating above the tree. This vision of beauty was dressed all in white holding a pearl Rosary. The children were in a joyful trance. Was this really happening to them?

Then the Lady spoke, "I come from Heaven. I have come to ask you to come here for six months on the thirteenth day of each month at this hour. Later I will tell you who I am and what I want." The children were spellbound. How sweet and kind she was. Their hearts were filled with tenderness. She also asked if they would sacrifice themselves for the conversion of sinners; they would suffer, but God would help them by granting His grace. They accepted her desires with deep fondness. They would do everything for this Lady of Grace. She also requested, "Pray the Rosary every day to bring peace to the world and the end of the war." Our wonderful little shepherds now knew the importance of prayer especially the Rosary. It was the story of Jesus' life. The more they prayed, the more they would realize the depth of His passion and the true meaning of life. Through their requested prayers, peace in the world would be realized.

In the ensuing appearances, the lovely Lady repeated her desire that the Rosary be prayed. The children lived her requests. They were so young and had such devoted hearts. How Jesus must love them! In July, the Lady showed the children a vision of the place where sinners go, and through their precious prayers and sacrifices sinners could be saved. Their hearts were engulfed in deep sadness and endless tears at seeing such a vision, which was devoid of God's presence. The exquisite Lady requested a devotion to her Immaculate Heart to help save these heartbreaking souls. How wonderful of God to have souls return to Him through the intercession of this beautiful Lady of Love. This must be Our Blessed Mary for her heart is overflowing with her love for God and for us. Our Father in Heaven is truly the essence of goodness and gives us the grace to live His life and return to His welcoming arms.

The Lady revealed who she was on Oct. 13, 1917. Seventy thousand people were present on that rainy, windy day. People were overwhelmed with excitement. Everyone wondered when the vision would appear. The children knelt down and began praying. Suddenly, there was the apparition of enchantment. They alone could see the incredible vision. The Lady spoke to Lucia and told her to continue to pray the Rosary, and then she said her holy name, "I am the Lady of the Rosary." What a revelation! This was the Mother of Jesus, Queen of the Rosary, Queen of Heaven, and God's Love. It was our irresistible Mary. Another request was that a chapel be built in her honor. People now could come to a consecrated place where they could pray and receive our beloved Jesus in Holy Communion. Mary could intercede for them, and give them our dear, sweet Lord's blessings. How wonderful!

Then Mary looked toward the sun, and the glorious sun began to dance, spin, and twirl on its axis. Suddenly, its golden hue turned to silver and began to zig zag towards earth in a myriad of rainbow colors shadowing everything in its path. It was coming closer and closer! Everyone was frightened! They feared it was the end of their Portugal! In one astonishing moment, the sun stopped its plunge to earth and returned safely to its home in the heavens. The people fell on their knees in awe, and gave thanks to God in jubilant prayer. As they looked around, many people were cured of their illnesses. What a moment in a lifetime that was to witness the wonders of that October day. The Lady that appeared to our little shepherds was truly Mary, and her son, Jesus, was performing spectacular miracles from Heaven. The awaited miracle had occurred that would give credibility to Mary's appearances to the children. Our Mother is always true to her words. Her love is eternal. Her heart is always glowing with tenderness for God's special family.

The children did not witness the miracle of the sun. They were in rapture as they witnessed revered and heavenly tableaus that they alone could see: St. Joseph giving a blessing while holding the Child Jesus, Our Mournful Lady of Dolors, Our Humble Lady of Mt. Carmel holding the holy scapular, and Our Divine Lord blessing the people in the Cova da Iria. What a fantastic miracle to see and share with each other at this moment in their lives. The miracle of the sun and the miracle of our Holy Family were seen as a reality in Fatima, Portugal. Now the children were believed, and faith grew in the hearts of the people. The memory of the woman "shining like the sun" would remain with them forever.

A quaint chapel was built where Mary appeared. It is known as the Apparition Chapel. Multitudes of pilgrims from near and distant places come and give love and affection to Jesus and Mary, and receive our Lord in the Holy Eucharist. Devotions to the Sacred Heart of Jesus and to the Immaculate Heart of Mary were embraced. The Rosary became part of people's hearts and was said with great dignity and affection. Fervent Rosary processions with a statue of Our Lady of Light were held day and night. A charming basilica, in addition to the chapel, was built to honor God, Jesus, and Mary.

Reconciliation and conversions occur in this land of Mary. It is so heart warming to see people fall more and more in love with Jesus and our splendid faith.

Jacinta and Francisco died at a very young age with Jesus in their hearts. Their experience with Our Blessed Mother inspired such a blazing devotion for her and for Jesus that they longed to be in Heaven with them. They truly were pure little saints. Lucia entered the convent of the Sisters of St. Dorothy and later became a

Carmelite nun. She gladly offered her life to our God and our eternal family and lived a life of total dedication. Lucia was privileged to see Our Lady from Heaven three more times in her different convents. Her heart was filled with such love to be in her presence once again.

Our Blessed Mary made certain requests to Lucia while at Fatima and again in her convents. They were revealed during the Second World War. They centered on: the consecration of Russia to her Immaculate Heart, attending our sacred Mass for the five first Saturdays of the month, and receiving our dear Jesus in the Holy Eucharist in reparation for sin committed against Mary's Immaculate Heart. God loved His Mary so much that He wanted all hurts committed against her be removed through the reception of the Eucharist. These wishes were an intricate part of Our Lady's heart and needed to be accomplished.

In 1942, Pope Pius XII consecrated the world to the Immaculate Heart of Mary and in 1952, he consecrated the people of Russia to her Immaculate Heart. The Bishops of the world were not involved in this decree. Our Blessed Mother's fervent desire was completely realized with Russia and the world being consecrated to her Immaculate Heart in 1984 by Pope John Paul II, in union with the world's bishops. The down fall of communism eventually occurred in the late 1980s. What a fantastic miracle, because for decades, communism had neither recognized our beautiful God nor our precious faith. Mary was the stimulus to end this evil, tyrannical form of government. The reparatory five first Saturdays emerged into a beautiful devotion.

Our Blessed Mother has said, "In the end my Immaculate Heart will triumph!" What a divine statement. With our love, devotion, and consecration to her Immaculate Heart, Mary will succeed. She desperately needs us to spread Jesus' faith and love, and return the world to God.

Mary's miraculous touch can bring the love, splendor and goodness of God to the world. Reconciliation and peace are the results. Lucia was immersed in Mary's heart and soul and lived her requests. How enchanting! Wherever our beautiful Mary appears, miracles happen. The world is inspired to ardently love our glorious faith. She is our Holy Mother and appears to us so that we might become one with Jesus' life of love, prayer, compassion, and forgiveness. Mary's requests, if lived, are our golden, spiritual staircase to attain Heaven.

Our Lady of Medjugorje

This miraculous story takes place in Yugoslavia, now known as Bosnia, Herzegovina, in the parish of Medjugorje. During the 1980s, the country was under communistic control. The faith-filled people of Medjugorje practiced their precious religion even though the atheistic view of life was ever present. They loved Jesus and Our Blessed Mother, and our God held them with fondness in His heart. The Catholic Croation children were raised in this grace-filled environment.

The country was very poor and farming was the main occupation. Vineyards and tobacco plants were intertwined in a rustic tapestry decorating the country side. Mountains encircled the vegetation and a serene, stoic beauty could be felt in the atmosphere.

It seems that out of poverty, where prayer is the center of peoples' lives, miracles occur. From miracles emerges grace and enriching faith, then the beauty and reality of God is revealed to us. Our Father is so caring, and He continuously offers us wonders. He has blessed this humble land with a gift that has touched the hearts of millions, and is offered to the whole world, if one opens their heart to faith.

The miracle of love began on June 24, 1981, in Bosnia Herzegovina. Two young ladies, Ivanka Ivankovic, fifteen-years-old, and Mirjana

Dragicevic, sixteen-years-old, were taking a stroll near their homes. They were enjoying the countryside conversing and appreciating the beauty of life. Suddenly, Ivanka noticed a brilliant, shinning light near the top of Mount Podbrdo, the rugged hill behind her village, Bijakovici. This locale is in the parish of Medjujorje. It startled and astonished her.

As she was transfixed looking at the hill, Ivanka saw a figure shimmering above the ground near its summit. With her heart beating wildly, Ivanka gazed intently at the lovely vision. It seemed to resemble a young woman. It looked like she was holding a baby. Could it be Mary, holding the Savior of the world? What a magnificent thought. She then said to her friend Mirjana, "Look, there is Gospa." That holy word has only one spectacular, incredible meaning in the Croatian language: "Our Lady." Mirjana believed Ivanka was joking, and in her wildest dreams could not visualize that Our Blessed Mother would ever appear to them. She didn't give it further thought and didn't even glance in that direction. Ivanka, at that moment, thought she too must have been seeing things, and they continued their friendly talk.

Later that day, their good friend Milka needed help rounding up her sheep. They were so pleased to assist her. These girls were all faith-filled girls and knew the meaning of friendship, caring, and helping each other. They tended to their sheep and as they were in the same vicinity of Mt. Podbrdo, they all looked up at the scenic hill. To their surprise, all three girls were engaged in seeing the enchanting Lady. With their hearts beating in nervous and frightened excitement, they fell to their knees and began praying. They could not believe their eyes. Was it a heavenly vision? Was it truly our Gospa? Their thoughts were spinning and their souls were filled with unbelievable love.

In time, another friend Vicka, greeted them and they said, "Look up there!" Vicka leapt in surprise at the mention of the incredible vision, and being very frightened, she quickly ran away. She met Ivan Ivankovick and Ivan Dragicevic and related the story to them. Being young men ready for any adventure, they quickly influenced Vicka to take them to the scene of the apparition. As they looked up at Mount Podbrdo, they all saw the charming Lady. It was a moment in a lifetime to be captured and held forever. Was this really occurring? Fear and love overcame them. They all went home in utter shock. Can you imagine the night these young people experienced?

The next day, June 25th, only four returned to the unique hill where they had seen the Lady. They were Ivanka Ivankovic, Mirjana Dragicevic, Ivan Dragicevic, and Vicka Ivankovic. Milka and Ivan Ivankovic, perhaps in fear, did not return where they had encountered the Lady, and therefore never again experienced the vision. Vicka in her excitement invited her friends, Marija Pavlovic, sixteen, and ten-year-old Jacov Colo, to accompany her and the others to see this vision of delight. There was such joy among these six friends. Their hearts were bursting with intense anticipation.

As they looked up at the hill, they saw a woman of indescribable beauty. She motioned to them to come to her. They rushed up to this Lady of Loveliness as if carried on wings of angels. As they came close to her, they knelt and prayed in irresistible joy. Their hearts were throbbing in awe. They went home that evening in wonderment.

On one of the following days when they returned, Mirjana asked the Lady who she was. She responded, "I am the Blessed Virgin Mary." What sacred words! What a revelation! It was Mary, Our Mother visiting Medjugorje, Herzegovina, on the other side of the world.

In the presence of ordinary, young people, Mary appears! Heaven speaks. God is always in our midst and gives us miracles constantly.

Later that same day Our Lady said to Marija, "Peace must reign between man and God and between all people."

Our Lady of Peace was giving us the secret to living God's endless love. We must immerse ourselves in Divine peace.

These six young people became the chosen group of visionaries that have been receiving messages from Our Mary for over three decades: Messages that involve making decisions concerning our soul, heart, and mind; Messages that give meaning and purpose to our life; Messages that will grant our salvation if lived.

The young visionaries in their own words described Our Lady "...as extremely beautiful, with dark hair, blue eyes, and rosy cheeks. She wears a gray dress and a white veil and has a crown of stars. She is pure love and brings immense grace. Little angels surround her." Imagine being in Our Lady's presence. It brings complete joy, a feeling of blessed love that overtakes one's whole being, a desire to always be with her forever. How filled with the Holy Spirit the visionaries were! How favored by Jesus they were!

The numerous messages that followed through Mary's many appearances are so poignant and intertwined with our gospels and church teachings. They center on love, faith, prayer, penance, fasting, the Rosary, reconciliation, conversion, and peace.

Our Lady has said, "Love" is the most important of all: love of God, love of Jesus, love of our faith, love of our family, love of our friends, love of our neighbor. To love is to live sharing ourselves. To love is to breathe goodness. To love is to forgive. To love is to always give. To love is to sacrifice. Ivan, one of the visionaries asked Our Blessed Mother why she was so beautiful. She answered, "Because I love." The secret of Our Lady's beauty is her interior "love" that shines from deep within her heart. We should try to imitate her always.

Some of Our Lady's other touching messages involve converting our lives, returning to God, living our faith, making the miracle of the Mass the center of our lives, praying with our hearts for our every need and concern, and praying for others so that prayer becomes the very essence of life. In prayer, we will come to love God more as our Father, our creator of life. We will be able to converse and relate our joys and sorrows, ask for his dear help, and thank Him for all His wonderful gifts given to us.

A beloved message that will raise us to the heights of love is that our hearts should become the home of the most Holy Trinity. We will then become devoted lovers of Jesus and live His life, sacraments, and eternal faith-filled love. We should consecrate ourselves passionately to the Sacred Heart of Jesus and the Immaculate Heart of Mary. How special to have our hearts melt into their beloved hearts. We are now experiencing Heaven on earth. If we live these inspired messages, we will experience an eternity of joy and love in God's warm caress.

St. James Church in Medjugorje has been the center of many apparitions of Our Blessed Mother to the visionaries. The Franciscan priests of St. James have witnessed the amazing fruits of Our Lady's appearances: Millions of people from every corner of the globe are attending Mass, receiving our Blessed Lord in the Holy Eucharist, and are experiencing deep joy and forgiveness in the sacrament of reconciliation. Many conversions are occurring. Fervent prayer groups are being established in various countries. Our faith is devotedly lived. People are filled with grace. Miracles of spiritual and physical healings are taking place. Our Blessed Mother is miraculously seen in the radiance of the sun. The golden sun has danced, wobbled, and twirled. Rainbows appeared when there was no burst of rain. Rosaries have turned a golden color. One of the most significant effects of Our Lady's presence is that people are saying the Rosary, which Our Lady of "pure love" has requested, and are receiving immeasurable blessings.

These miraculous appearances of Our Blessed Mother and remarkable occurrences have been going on for many precious years, in our world, in our time. Aren't these exceptional miracles of love? Only God can give us such blessings.

Presently, Ivanka sees Our Blessed Mother once a year on June 25th, the anniversary of the first apparition to the six visionaries. She looks forward to seeing her Mother of Joy. Mirjana sees her on March 18th, her birthday, and Mary appears to Mirjana on the second of every month. She misses her daily conversations with Our Lady of the Mountain, but her heart and soul belong to Mary and Jesus. Jacov has the privilege of seeing Our Mother on Dec. 25th, Christmas. What a magnificent day to be in Our Lady's presence. Vicka, Ivan and Marija continue to have daily visions. They are so thankful and consumed in Our Lady's love. On the third Thursday of the month, Marija tells her priest at St. James Our Blessed Mother's message, and he relates it to the world. What blessed revelation given to God's children. Mary continues to lavish her affection on all of her dear visionaries and on us!

More than thirty million people have visited Medjugorje and have fallen in love with Mary and her beloved Son, Jesus. She is our sweet Mother and has called herself "the Queen of Peace." Our Blessed Mother has bestowed overpowering grace and divine splendor on Medjugorje. She has transformed our world through her appearances. Mary wants us to live her Son's precious gospels and live our faith! She is beckoning us to fall deeply in love with God and return to Him.

These are a few messages in Our Lady's own words that reveal her powerful love!

December 25, 1998

"Dear children! Today, on the birthday of my Son, my heart is filled with immeasurable joy, love, and peace. As your mother, I desire in each of you that same joy, peace, and love in your heart. That is why do not be afraid to open your heart and to completely surrender yourself to Jesus, because only in this way can he enter your heart and fill it with love, peace, and joy. I bless you with my motherly blessing."

May 25, 2000

"Dear children, I rejoice with you and in this time of grace, I call you to spiritual renewal. Pray, little children that the Holy Spirit may come to dwell in you in fullness, so that you may be able to witness in joy to all those that are far from the faith. Especially, little children, pray for the gifts of the Holy Spirit so that in the spirit of love, every day and in each situation, you may be close to your fellowman; and that in wisdom and love you may overcome every difficulty. I am with you and I intercede for each of you before Jesus. Thank you for having responded to my call."

June 25, 2009

"Dear children! Rejoice with me, convert in joy and give thanks to God for the gift of my presence among you. Pray that in your hearts, God may be the center of your life and with your life give witness, little children, so that every creature may feel God's love. Be my extended hands for every creature so that they may grow closer to the God of love. I bless you with my motherly blessing. Thank you for having responded to my call."

February 25, 2010

"Dear Children, In this time of grace, when nature also prepares to give the most beautiful colors of the year, I call you dear children to open your hearts to God the Creator for Him to transform you and mold you in His image, so that all the good that has fallen asleep in your hearts may awaken to a new life and a longing towards eternity. Thank you for having responded to my call."

July 25, 2010

"Dear Children! Anew I call you to follow me with joy. I desire to lead all of you to my Son, your Savior. You are not aware that without Him you do not have joy and peace, nor a future or eternal life. Therefore, make good use of this time of joyful prayer and surrender. Thank you for having responded to my call."

April 25, 2014

"Dear Children, Open your hearts to the grace which God is giving you through me, as a flower opens to the warmth of the sun. Be prayer and love to all those that are far from God and His love. I am with you and intercede for all of you before my son Jesus and I love you with immeasurable love. Thank you for having responded to my call."

Mary appears and miracles happen. If we listen to her heart and compelling messages, salvation is ours! Her heart beats with love for us. Our adorable Lady of "pure love" wants to share God and Jesus with us for eternity. It is up to us to respond!

As for me the answer to Mary is Yes, Yes, Yes, I'll live your messages! I'll live Jesus' life of "Love."

Tapestry of Love

God created a very special world and accentuated its beauty with living creatures. Then in the midst of this glory, He created man and woman with a soul, an intellect, and free will. He gifted us with His beloved Son, His Holy Spirit, and His treasured Mary. Jesus in His passionate love for us became man to redeem us, and teach us to love. Mary returns to us to urge, inspire, and lead us to Jesus who will help us to journey home, to our Father in Heaven. The apparitions of our endearing Mary are a tapestry of love to escort us to God's divine embrace.

To Juan Diego Our Blessed Mother said, "Know and be certain in your heart, my precious Son, that I am the Ever Virgin Holy Mary, Mother of the One, true God Who created Heaven and Earth." She bestowed on us her engaging image on Juan's tilma and through her intercession to our Savior, conversions and miracles occurred. Our Lady of Guadalupe Church was built on Tepeyac Hill. In today's spectacular basilica, millions of people visit each year and receive Jesus in the Holy Eucharist – faith is renewed.

To Giovanni Chichizola Our Lady said, "Don't be afraid Giovanni. I am Mary the Mother of God. Tell the people of Rapallo that you have seen me." We received the incredible icon of her Assumption and deep faith emerged and was faithfully lived. Our Lady of Montallegro Church was built and Jesus was adored.

Sister Catherine Labouré's guardian angel said to her in the convent of the Daughters of Charity, "The Blessed Virgin awaits you." After several encounters with Sister Catherine, Our Blessed Mother instructed her to have a precious medal made that would give graces to those who wear it with confidence. The Miraculous Medal was given to the world and healings, conversions, and a multitude of miracles ensued.

To Bernadette Soubirous Our Mother of Love said, "I am the Immaculate Conception." Our Mary has given us proof of her conception free from original sin and her blessed Motherhood of Jesus. She also gifted us with her miraculous spring. Countless miracles were the result. The Lourdes Chapel and Basilica were built, and people fell more in love with Jesus in the Holy Eucharist and with his cherished Mother.

To Lucia, Francisco, and Jacinta, Our Blessed Lady said, "I am the Lady of the Rosary." Our Mary gave us the spiritual importance and effect of saying the Rosary especially for peace in the world. She asked for devotion to her Immaculate Heart and her devotion has been gloriously enacted. Our Blessed Mother has said, "In the end my Immaculate Heart will triumph." What splendid words to give us hope and assurance that Jesus will reign in our world with Mary as Our Queen. The "miracle of the sun" in Fatima is a testimony of God's favor on Mary, for the laws of physics were denied, and proof of God's presence was fervently felt. The request made to Lucia that Russia be consecrated to the Immaculate Heart of Mary was fully accomplished, and the fall of communism occurred. What incredible happenings.

To Mirjana the exquisite Lady said, "I am the Blessed Virgin Mary" and the visionaries were spellbound in love. The multitude of messages given to Ivanka, Mirjana, Vicka, Ivan, Marija, and Jacov focus on: love, faith, prayer, fasting, reconciliation, conversion, peace, and praying the Rosary. They inspire us to love God, Jesus, the Holy Spirit, and Mary with overwhelming devotion. We are to live our holy faith in God's presence and return to His welcoming arms.

Mary appears and we become saturated in love! Her visits to earth weave a magnificent tapestry that is continually evolving to touch our souls to live in Jesus' love and bring us to our destined home. Mary's apparitions are a splendid reality. Bernadette related to us so charmingly that she could only give us the messages and that it is up to us to believe.

I have given you the miracle of Mary's appearances in this book, written in love. It is up to you to believe. The choice is yours! As for me, I believe! Our magnificent Mary has captured my heart!

Bibliography

Connell, Janice—The Visions Of The Children; The Apparitions of the Blessed Mother at Medjugorje—St. Martin's Press, New York 1992

Connell, Janice T.—Queen of the Cosmos: Interviews with the Visionaries of Medjugorje—Paraclete Press, Brewster, Massachusetts 1990, revised edition, 2004

Delany John J. editor—A Woman Clothed With the Sun—Image Books, Garden City, New York, 1961

Medjugorje Magazine: editors and publishers, —Larry and Mary Eck, Westmont, Illinois, Spring 2010

Lord, Bob and Penny—The Many Faces of Mary a love story—Journeys of Faith, Bob and Penny Lord, Morrilton, Arkansas, 1987

Lovasik, Lawrence Rev. S.V.D.—Our Heavenly Mother—Catholic Book Publishing CO. New Jersey, 1997

Mullen, Peter—Shrines of Our Lady—St. Martin's Press, New York, 1998

Nolan Denis-Medjugorje And The Church—Queenship Publishing, Goleta, California, 1995

Odell, Catherine M.—Those Who Saw Her: Apparitions of Mary—Our Sunday Visitor Publishing Division, Huntington, Indiana 1995

http://www.indefenseofthecross.com/apparitions.htm

http://www.mediugorie.org/msg10.htm

Made in the USA
San Bernardino, CA
16 September 2018